Walkthrough

Let's look at the front cover of our book. Can anyone read the title to us by sounding out and blending all through the words? Read the title. What do you hink is ponging?

honic Opportunity

le of the book rhymes. Which words rhyme?

The Pong Song

What happens when the pong is too strong?

Walkthrough

Let's have a look at the back cover. What is chasing Dad? Let's read the blurb. Read and discuss the blurb.

Walkthrough

Let's look at the title page. Can you see what might be making the 'pong'?

Phonic Opportunity

Look at the title. Which letters are making the rhyme in the title? Point to the letter string '-ong'.

Walkthrough

What can we see in the picture? Role-play the word 'sniffing'. Can you think of a word that rhymes with 'sniffing'?

Sniffing, whiffing socks.

2

Observe and Prompt

Word Recognition

Encourage the children to use their decoding skills to sound out and blend the phonemes to read the words. If children struggle with 'sniffing' and 'whiffing', tell them these words and model reading them.

Walkthrough

Take the children's suggestions for other words that rhyme with 'sniffing' and introduce 'whiffing'.

Observe and Prompt

Language Comprehension

- Check that the children understand that the socks are smelly.
- Encourage the children to read the words with expression.

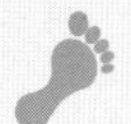

Walkthrough

What are Dad's trainers doing? Do you know a nursery rhyme about a mouse that ran up the clock? Say the nursery rhyme *Hickory Dickory Dock* together.

Observe and Prompt

Word Recognition

P Check that the children are reading the words using their decoding skills, sounding out and blending through each word.

- If children struggle with 'trainers', tell them this word, and model how to sound out and blend through the word to read it.

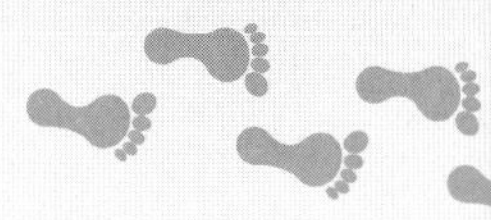

Observe and Prompt

Language Comprehension

- Check that the children understand that this text is a different version of a well-known rhyme.
- What do the children think might happen next?

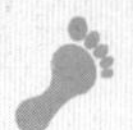

Walkthrough

What do you do if there's a pong?
What is the clock doing here?
Why can't the clock 'bong'?

The clock won't bong.

6

Observe and Prompt

Word Recognition

- (P) Check that the children are using their decoding skills to read the words 'clock', 'bong', 'pong's' and 'strong'.
- If the children struggle with 'won't', tell them this word.

The pong's too strong.

7

Observe and Prompt

Language Comprehension

- Can children describe how the clock is feeling, and why?

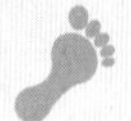

Walkthrough

How is the clock feeling now?

Observe and Prompt

Word Recognition

- (P) Encourage the children to use their decoding skills to sound out and blend through 'ticking', 'tocking' and 'shock'.
- If they struggle with the two-syllable words or with 'What', tell them these words.

Language Comprehension

- Encourage the children to compare the text with *Hickory Dickory Dock.*

Walkthrough

What is huffing and puffing in this picture?

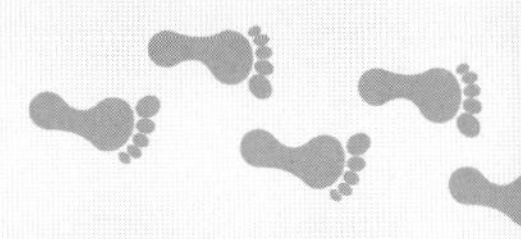

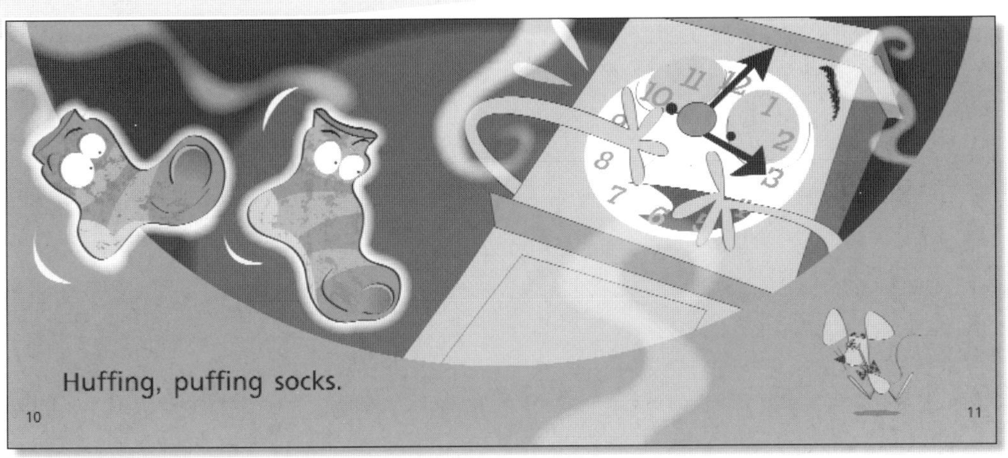

Observe and Prompt

Word Recognition

P Encourage the children to use their decoding skills to read the words, and help them if they struggle with the two-syllable words.

Language Comprehension

- What do the children think might happen next?

Walkthrough

What are the trainers doing now? What are the socks doing? How do you think this makes the clock feel?

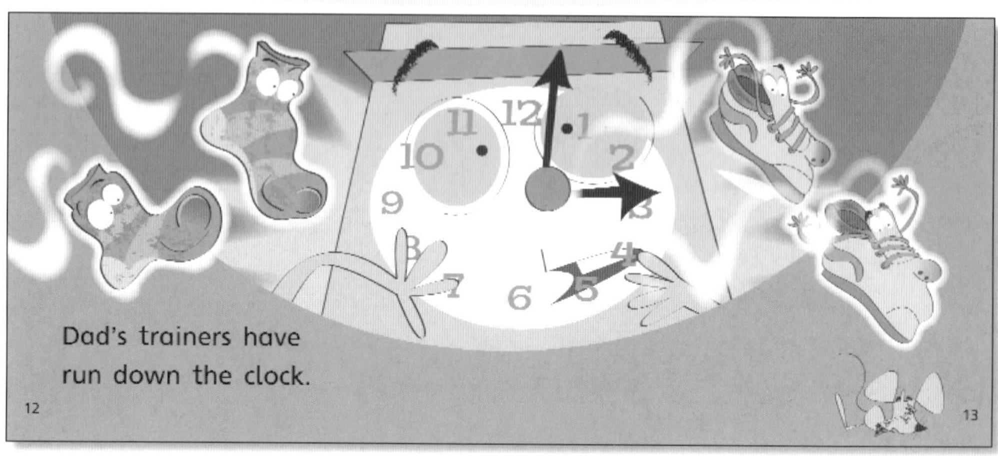

Observe and Prompt

Word Recognition

- (P) Check that the children sound out and blend all through the words 'Dad's', 'run' and 'clock'.
- If the children struggle with the other words, tell them these words and model how to use decoding skills to read them.

Language Comprehension

- Encourage the children to talk about the story and explain what is happening.

Walkthrough

The trainers have gone mad, haven't they? What are they doing to poor Dad? Why do you think they are doing this?

Observe and Prompt

Word Recognition

- (P) Encourage children to use decoding skills to sound out and blend all through the words 'mad' and 'Dad'.
- If the children struggle with the other words, tell them these words and model reading them.

Language Comprehension

- What do the children think might happen next?

Walkthrough

What is happening now? Look – the trainers are chasing Dad round the block!

(You may need to explain 'block'.)

Observe and Prompt

Word Recognition

- Check that children use their decoding skills to sound out and blend the phonemes all through the word 'block'.
- Check that children can recognise and independently read the sight words 'him' and 'the'.
- The other words may not be decodable for all children at this stage. If they struggle, tell them these words and model using decoding skills to read them.